FROM BROKENNESS TO BLESSING

A Collection of Poetry by
VICTORIA ASHBY

FROM BROKENNESS TO BLESSING © 2017
by Victoria Ashby

Paperback – ISBN: 978-0-9934910-7-8

All rights reserved.
No part of this publication may be reproduced, stored in a retrieval system, or transmitted in any form or by any means, electronic, mechanical, photocopying or otherwise, without prior written consent of the publisher except as provided by under United Kingdom copyright law. Short extracts may be used for review purposes with credits given.

Copyright permissions

Scripture quotations from The Authorized (King James) Version. Rights in the Authorized Version in the United Kingdom are vested in the Crown. Reproduced by permission of the Crown's patentee, Cambridge University Press.

THE HOLY BIBLE, NEW INTERNATIONAL VERSION®, NIV® Copyright © 1973, 1978, 1984, 2011 by Biblica, Inc.® Used by permission. All rights reserved worldwide.

Published by
Maurice Wylie Media
Bethel Media House
Tobermore
Magherafelt
Northern Ireland
BT45 5SG (UK)

Publishers' statement: Throughout this book the love for our God is such that whenever we refer to Him we honour with Capitals. On the other hand, when referring to the devil, we refuse to acknowledge him with any honour to the point of violating grammatical rule and withholding capitalisation.

For more information visit
www.MauriceWylieMedia.com

Endorsement

It is my great pleasure to recommend this beautiful book of poems. Here you will find raw emotion, honesty, struggle and pain. All wonderfully meeting hope, peace and the rescue and love of our wonderful Saviour.

Pastor Alistair Ritchie

Contents

'Stay'	9
'Changed'	13
'Held'	23
'Worthy'	27
'Broken'	32
'Words'	37
'Scarred'	41
'Encouraged'	47
'Free'	50
'Forgiven'	58
'Trust'	63
'Storms'	69
'Loved'	74
'Time'	80
'Complete'	85

Introduction

These words have been written down from my heart and my soul. They tell the story of a young woman who has been through darkness beyond her years, who has felt worthless and alone. A young woman who thought she had no purpose and felt rejected by a lot of people in her life. But, Jesus turned that right around. As being this young woman, I met Him when I was at my lowest and He heard my desperate cries of brokenness. He was the only one able to help me. Through His acceptance of me, by His love and grace, He has changed my life forever.

It's in those moments of prayer when seeking Him that these poems and verses were penned. Poetry is a release for me, it is an expression of my soul singing. The poems in this book share the heartache, highs and lows which I have experienced in my life. Through the darkness, God has guided me, without Him I am nothing. Whether you find yourself in darkness or in light, I hope the words in this book will help your journey in grace, His hand is with you, His direction is clear to guide you. The life I live now is a life in surrender to Jesus. It is because of Him that this book exists and I use it for His power and His glory. It is written out of love, from a thankful heart to praise, worship and glorify Him.

May these pages be more than words, may they sing to you, may they make music in your heart and draw you closer into our Lord Jesus Christ, who has turned my life 'From Brokenness to Blessing!'

I came into Your presence,
You had heard my call,
And in that precious moment,
It was as if, I'd never been away at all.

I came to You broken,
I had wandered far away,
But You were pleased to see me,
You didn't turn me away.

I came to You heavy laden,
My life was such a mess,
Yet You took all my troubles,
You gave me peace and rest.

I came to You ashamed
Of all the things I'd done,
But You had already forgiven me,
By sacrificing Your Son.

I came to You with sadness,
Tears streaming from my eyes,
You put Your arms around me,
You took away all satan's lies.

I came to You feeling lost and helpless,
In shame, I turned my face away,
But You whispered: "My child, I love you."
You whispered to me: "Stay."

Changed...

From Brokenness to Blessing

My past will always haunt me
Like a ghost that cannot rest.
My soul it is in turmoil,
My heart can never rest.

I hear the voices every day
That speak the words of old,
About how I am nothing,
I feel so tired and cold.

My thoughts are always of hatred,
Which I turn against myself,
Why can I not get past it?
Is this the card I have been dealt?

Never to feel respected,
Never to be loved,
Never to mean something or
have a purpose,
Why can't I rise above?

Will nobody help me?
Will no one hear my call?
Is my life just meaningless and empty?
Would the world miss me at all?

Yet, in that moment of desperation,
I can feel Your touch.
You have come to hold me
And tell me, You love me so much.

You silence the voices,
You help to ease the pain.
And in that special moment,
I know I will never be the same!

"My Child, why do you feel such sorrow?
Why are you so blue?
Surely you know I love you,
And I've always wanted you."

"Did you forget about Me?
If you'd only called My name,
I'd have come to you much sooner
And brought you back again."

"Back into My presence,
Where there is only love and care,
Why do you carry such burdens alone
When you know I Am here to share?"

Changed...

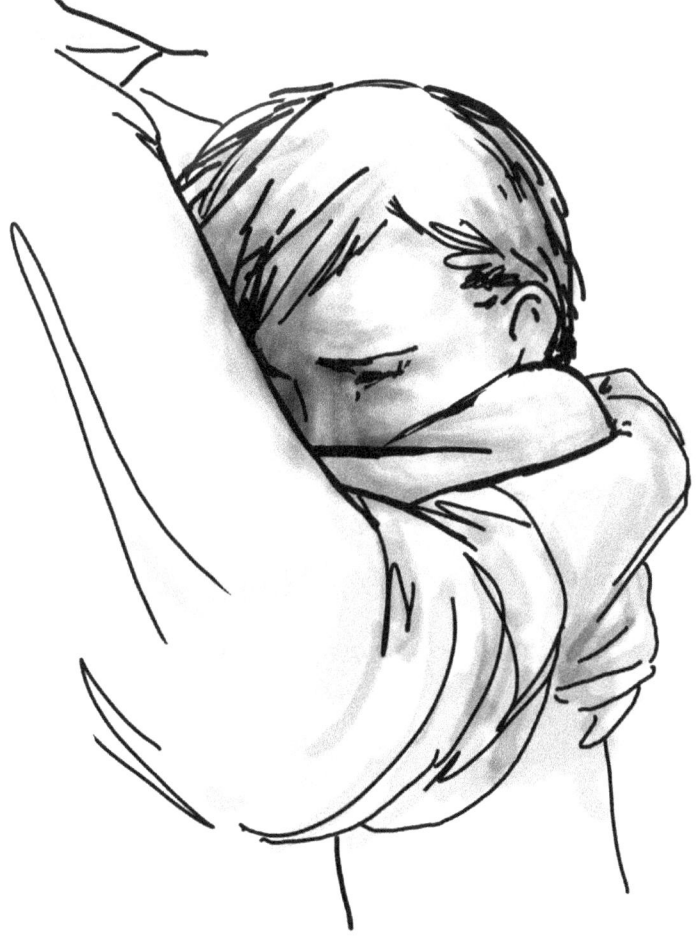

"To Me you are worth everything,
I even gave My only Son.
To show how much I love you,
What more could I have done?"

You put Your arms around me,
You take away my fear,
You hold me forever,
You wipe away my tears.

The darkness flashes away,
I enter into the light,
The feeling of inadequacy,
I no longer must fight.

I realise how much time I've wasted
In feeling all those things untrue,
When all I had to do
Was give it all to You.

"Humble yourselves therefore under the mighty hand of God, that he may exalt you in due time: Casting all your care upon him; for he careth for you."

1 Peter 5:6-7

Held...

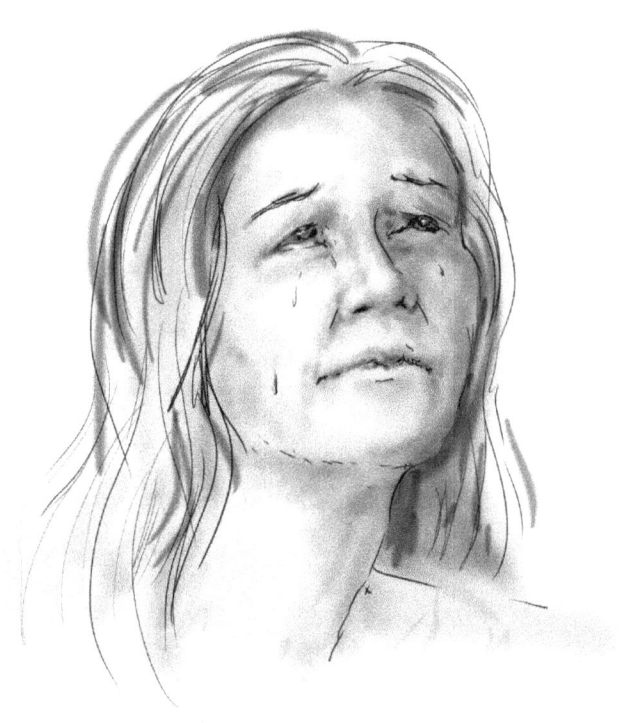

When your heart is troubled and full of pain
and you feel you can never be the same.
Just call upon His name...
He cares for you.

When the sunshine's gone and there's only rain
and your soul is full of sorrow and shame,
And you don't know how you will
make it through again...
He cares for you.

When the tears come streaming
down your face.
And you feel you will never win the race,
Just remember His love and grace…
He cares for you.

When you feel so all alone and you don't
have the strength on your own.
He will always bring you home…
He cares for you.

*And when that final day arrives and we
rise to meet Him in the skies,
And we have overcome all satan's lies...
He cares for you.*

Worthy...

You have made me worthy
Because I am loved by You.
I have been forgiven,
I have unlocked the truth.

I have sense and purpose
Because I called upon Your name.
I have entered into Your presence,
You took my sin and shame.

The emptiness I felt inside
Is now full of joy and song.
I want to be in Your presence,
Feeling close to You all day long.

I've received such blessings
Since You came into my life.
All the past has melted away,
Free from worry and strife.

I live rest assured in Your promises
And in Your unfailing love.
"Oh, what a Saviour!"
The angels sing from above.

I cannot wait to be with You
In my final place of rest.
To be in Your presence,
To finally see Your face.

Worthy...

*And when the book is opened
On that Judgement day,
The pages will be empty
Because You have washed it all away.*

For what shall it profit

a man, if he shall gain the

whole world, and lose

his own soul?

Mark 8:36 KJV

Broken...

Broken...

*I have been broken,
In ways you will never know.
My heart has been crushed,
There is rejection in my soul.*

*I have felt lonely,
Like there is no one but me,
Wandering through this darkness,
Without a light to see.*

I have felt unworthy,
Like on this planet I don't belong.
There is no joy, there is no hope,
I can never sing a song.

But that is where You meet me,
The wonderful I Am.
You reach down and touch me,
In ways no one else can.

You minister unto me,
You heal my broken heart.
You fill me with Your joy,
You give me a new start.

You walk with me through shadows,
You give me peace and rest.
You make me feel so loved,
Like only a father can show best.

All those feelings of emptiness fall from
my mind, like the waves of the sea.
For You have come to meet me,
You have rescued me.

Now I will never be lonely,
I will never feel unloved.
Because for ever and ever,
I'm a child of the Lord above.

Words...

Words can hurt and words can heal,
Words can love and words can steal.
Words can wound this heart of mine,
So please try not to be unkind.

A harsh word lives on, long after it is spoken.
A heart is hard to piece back together,
once it has been broken.

Words can be forgiven,
Even ones vulgar and rotten.
But their sting can live on forever,
They are not easily forgotten.

So next time we open up our mouths,
Let's think before we speak.
Let us not be angry, let us not be weak.

Instead of wanting to shout and scream,
To maim and hurt and scare.
Why don't you look to God above?
And take it to Him in prayer.

From Brokenness to Blessing

A gentle answer turns
away wrath, but a harsh
word stirs up anger.

The tongue of the wise adorns
knowledge, but the mouth of the
fool gushes folly.

The eyes of the Lord are
everywhere, keeping watch
on the wicked and the good.

The soothing tongue is a tree of
life, but a perverse tongue crushes
the spirit.

Proverbs 15:1-5 NIV

Scarred...

I hate how you made me hate me,
How your words have left a scar.
How what you did has haunted me,
From my mind, it's never far.

I hate the words you spoke over me,
That caused me so much pain.
I hate that forever,
I felt, I was to blame.

Scarred...

I hate that you have influenced
The person I've become.
The anger and hurt in my heart
Has left me rather numb.

I hate that I've felt worthless
For so very long.
I hate I didn't get the help
I needed all along.

I hate that I never realised
The fault was always with you,
And that everything you said to me,
None of it was true.

I hate that I didn't realise
I should not take the blame,
For I was just a pawn
In your sick and twisted game.

I hate that I wasted tears on you,
It makes me really mad.
And all those wasted years of sorrow
Has left me feeling sad.

It took a lot to realise
The responsibility lies at your door.
It was nothing I did and not
what I deserved,
I no longer feel sore.

My smile is back, my soul has healed.
My heart has learned to beat.
How did I get through this?
I've learned to leave it at
the Master's feet.

Encouraged...

Sometimes life can get you down,
You fight to smile instead of frown.
The tiredness and the sickness
takes control,
The joy has left your troubled soul.

But in the midst of worries or cares,
The Faithful one will always be there.
To draw us close when we need a friend,
His courage and strength,
He will always lend.

Encouraged...

*And the things that once seemed
to be so blue,
Fade away when I give them to You.*

*For this is the only way
I can face another day.*

Free...

Free...

The fakeness of my smile deceives you,
The skills of my act are great.
The cracks smothered over by laughter,
When inside, I'm ready to break.

The secret tears slide silently down
And linger on my cheek.
I cry alone in the darkness
Where everything is bleak.

No one notices as I withdraw inwards,
As the light, it fades to grey.
I nod and smile just enough to conceal
And silently slip away.

From Brokenness to Blessing

They wouldn't understand me,
My heart is so full of pain.
My heart is so broken and battered,
Will I ever be the same?

The pieces won't fit back together,
No matter how hard I try.
This life has left me exhausted,
Sometimes I wish I could die!

Would anybody miss me?
Would they even care,
If one day I just disappeared
And was no longer there?

My life no longer a burden,
A load too heavy to bear.
A lonely road I walk upon,
My grief has no one with which to share.

A life so empty and meaningless,
A heart so dead and cold.
How to love, it has forgotten,
My soul feels so very old.

But at that point of desperation,
I hear a voice whisper in my ear.
"My child it's Me, your Creator,
You have nothing left to fear."

"In you I take pleasure,
For you I gave my life.
Let Me take your burdens,
Let Me take your strife."

"For I am the potter,
And you are the clay,
I have moulded and shaped you,
I have made you this way."

"To Me you are beautiful,
No matter how blemished or wild.
Because I am your Father,
And you will always be My child."

"Don't give up hope, My daughter,
I'm not finished with you yet.
For you will be like the purest gold,
For you, I paid the debt."

"For you're still a work in progress
And the race may be long and hard,
But in the end will be perfection,
When I meet you in the clouds."

Suddenly my heart lifted,
It began to beat.
The tears replaced by joy
As I fell down at your feet.

I realised I am special,
In every single way.
And this is what I cling to,
To get me through each day.

For You don't look at my failures,
Or the battles lost or won,
You merely see the face
of Your beloved Son.

It's in Your promises I cling to,
And in Your arms I stay.
For there You will keep me safe from harm
Until that wondrous day.

Free...

*That day I will go to be with You
And by Your side I will stay
In that beautiful promised paradise,
For ever and a day!*

Then we which are alive and remain
shall be caught up together
with them in the clouds,
to meet the Lord in the air: and so
shall we ever be with the Lord.

1 Thessalonians 4:17 KJV

Forgiven...

It was not the nails that held Him
Upon that rugged tree,
But it was the Father's love
For the likes of you and me.

It was not the lashes
That caused him the pain,
But our rejection of His Father
And yet He took the blame.

It was not the spitting nor the mocking
That made Him want to cry,
But the painful denial of His purpose
By the likes of you and I.

It was not the stone that kept Him
In that tomb until that day,
But the casting away of all our sin,
It was the only way.

But it was His love for His Father
That made Him want to stay,
And face that brutal execution,
He didn't run away.

So why do we keep running
When such a sacrifice was made?
It has cost us nothing
And yet His punishment seems to fade.

To most it's unimportant,
To some it's just a tale.
Some don't even know it's true,
They think God's love is for sale.

It was not the crown of thorns
That made Him a King.
It was the message He was trying to impart,
Salvation for us to bring.

So what is stopping you?
Why with your old life won't you part?
Why won't you accept Him,
And make Him King of your heart?

It was not the nails that held Him
On that awful cross,
But it was His love for us,
So we do not have to suffer loss.

He gave us the greatest gift,
The one that's free to all.
The gift of unconditional love,
If we just hear His call.

Trust...

From Brokenness to Blessing

The voices in my head keep taunting me
With things that are not true.
Trying to create a distance
Between me and You.

It's sad, sometimes I listen
To the lies they have to tell,
Even when I know the truth,
My soul, they would sell.

Why do I listen to such lies
That whisper in my ear?
They take away all my peace
And create a sense of fear.

Trust...

Oh Father, why do I give into temptation?
Why am I so weak?
Why do I find it so difficult to pray
And trust and seek?

The solace of my Father,
Whose blood has covered me,
Who has planned and mapped my life
With the things I cannot see.

Why do I find it so difficult to trust You,
When the way I cannot see?
Even though I know, if only I follow,
No harm will come to me.

Why do I always question You,
When Your will I already know?
Instead of simply obeying,
And being ready and willing to go.

Why do I find it so frustrating,
When I do not understand,
Something I am not meant to?
Instead of just believing in Your hand.

Teach me Lord to simply follow You
And not to look around.
Teach me to listen to Your voice,
A welcome and familiar sound.

Why do I not speak the truth
To banish away the fear?
For all I have to do is call Your name,
And the great I Am is near.

Oh teach me Lord to trust You,
In everything I do,
Teach me not to wander,
Far away from You.

Teach me not to listen
To things that are not good,
Instead help me to love and follow You,
Like every good daughter should.

From Brokenness to Blessing

For I know the plans
I have for you,
declares the Lord,
plans to prosper you
and not to harm you,
plans to give you hope
and a future.

Jeremiah 29:11 NIV

Storms...

From Brokenness to Blessing

The storms of life have broken
and battered me,
And now I'm drowning in the sea.
The sea of regret and shame,
I only have myself to blame.

I turned my back on all things good,
Refused to live life as I should,
And now the sun has gone and
there is only rain,
And all I have is, sorrow and pain.

There's only darkness, I can't find
the light. The world is grey,
I've lost my sight.
I'm crying out in despair,
Will anybody hear my prayer?

But in that moment, You calm the sea.
You come down and meet with me,
You minister Your love and grace,
I hide from You, my guilty face!

You speak: "Child I'm here, I never went
away, it was you who wandered,
it was you who strayed.
Come back to me now, I welcome you,
I will cleanse and make you new!"

And from that moment I can truly say,
My burdens have been rolled away.
The sea is calm, the sun is out,
Tears of joy my heart doth shout!

Storms...

Your grace has washed it all away,
You've given me a new start
and a brand-new day.
You have captured my soul,
Your touch has made me whole.

I cannot keep this to myself,
I want no riches, status or wealth.
Only to praise and glorify Your name,
For I will never be the same.

Loved...

Loved...

You knew me before my life began,
You loved me before my lungs filled with air,
You made me beautiful in your image,
There was nothing lovelier or more fair.

You have walked beside me throughout everything,
the good times and the bad.
You guided me when I felt lost
And held me when I was hurt or sad.

When I couldn't see a way forward,
You gave me the light to see.
And when I was too weak to walk,
It was then You carried me.

When I felt I couldn't hear Your voice,
It was then You whispered in my ear.
And when I felt all alone,
It was then that You drew near.

Oh what a Father You have been to me,
There is no greater friend.
I know I will always be Your child,
Until the very end.

You have done all this for me,
You have set me apart.
And yet all in return You ask,
Is for me to give my heart.

My freedom was paid with such a price,
How could I refuse?
Oh yes, My Jesus, take my heart,
My life is Yours to use.

And as I walk this path of life,
May I, a good example be.
May my life be a witness,
May the world see You through me!

Loved...

I am crucified with Christ:
nevertheless I live; yet not I,
but Christ liveth in me: and the life
which I now live in the
flesh I live by the faith of the
Son of God, who loved me,
and gave himself for me.

Galations 2:20 KJV

Time...

Time...

You say you're far too busy
To waste time on the things above,
The thought of church makes you uneasy,
you don't care about His love.

You say you have plenty of time
But life's clock continues to tick away,
Why put off until tomorrow
Something you need to address today?

You say your life is great,
Though you look a little lost,
Not sure of your direction,
Not considering the cost.

You say: "I'll do it when I'm older!"
But it comes in the blink of an eye,
Please stop and listen,
Don't let the chance pass you by.

You say: "I've tried religion,
It didn't work for me."
But that's not what salvation is about,
He died to set you free.

You say: "It's just not for me."
Turn your back and walk away.
But what if tomorrow never comes
And you face the Judgement day.

You say there is no reason to life,
You're here and then you're gone,
The truth is just a story,
You won't consider you are wrong.

But my friend, wouldn't it be sad,
When all is said and done,
If you wasted the opportunity,
To receive the Son.

For you might have success and riches,
This worldly life may make you feel whole.
But wouldn't it be sad
If you paid for it with your soul.

For what has man to gain?
He is not in control,
It's the Heavenly realm that matters,
Have you considered your soul?

For on that day when He returns,
And the book is opened and read,
Wouldn't it be sad
If the Holy One said:

"Depart from Me, I never knew you,
I cannot make you whole
And now amid excuses,
You have lost your soul."

Complete...

I had looked everywhere for love,
In all the wrong places,
Searching for something real,
Finding only lies and false faces.

Thinking I could find it in a person
But my search, it was in vain.
Finding only broken promises,
Leading to a heart full of scars and pain.

I had looked everywhere for acceptance,
For the person that I am,
Finding only disappointment and rejection,
In a world that does not give a damn!

I had tried everything to fill the void,
The deep hole in my soul,
But nothing I tried could satisfy,
Nothing could make me whole.

Then I realised it was not a person that
I needed, that no single human
could bridge that gap,
It was only true love from a Father above,
That could release me from this trap.

It was only Jesus who could make me see
I am beautiful to Him.
He has washed me clean
And banished away my sin!

He has accepted me
When the world had let me down.
He has filled me with His love and mercy,
He has given me a crown!

He has made me realise
What true love is all about.
Now I have become complete,
He took the pain and doubt.

Now I do not need the world's acceptance,
Or love of man or human friend,
Because I am His daughter,
His true love, loves me to the end.

Complete...

And I will never be lonely,
Even though I walk in a world
that is dark and sad,
Because I have accepted the Saviour,
He is the best friend and Father,
I have ever had!

He never forgot or rejected me,
Even when I was tarnished from sin.
Oh no! He gladly received me,
And I let Him enter in.

And now my life is so different,
There are no let downs, scars or pain,
Instead just peace and love,
Even through the storms and the rain.

Oh friend, do not waste time
on the things of earth,
For they will only make you frown,
But put your trust in the Master,
For He will never let you down!

All He wants is to love you,
All He asks is for your heart,
It is only Him who can complete you
And give you a fresh start.

So why do you not come to Him,
He says; "Cast your cares on Me!"
He will make you whole again
And He will set you free!
To God be the glory!

Complete...

Jesus Christ the same
yesterday, and
to day, and for ever.

Hebrews 13:8 KJV

Special thanks to...

Firstly, to my family, for the encouragement and support that they have always provided to me.

Also, my pastor's Alistair Ritchie and Bill Foye, and my friends in Hope Church, Hillsborough, for their unconditional support and spiritual encouragement.

I am proud to serve alongside you.

To the Maurice Wylie Media publishing team, who took what I could not see and made it plain for all to see.

And finally, but most importantly, to my amazing Saviour, Jesus Christ. It is because of Your sacrifice and love that I found me. Let this book be a token of praise to a Father who took a vessel that was helpless and unworthy, making it shiny and new.

INSPIRED TO WRITE A BOOK?
Contact
Maurice Wylie Media
Inspirational Christian Publisher

Based in Northern Ireland and distributing across the world
www.MauriceWylieMedia.com

www.ingramcontent.com/pod-product-compliance
Lightning Source LLC
Chambersburg PA
CBHW070547300426
44113CB00011B/1814